READING TUDOR AND STUART HANDWRITING

Lionel Munby

Alphabet drawn by Phillip Judge

Published by PHILLIMORE for
BRITISH ASSOCIATION FOR LOCAL HISTORY
with the aid of a grant from the
Calouste Gulbenkian Foundation

1988

Published for
BRITISH ASSOCIATION FOR LOCAL HISTORY
by PHILLIMORE & CO. LTD.
Shopwyke Hall, Chichester, Sussex

ISBN 0 85033 638 4

Printed by Chichester Press Limited.

Contents

Illustrations

Alphabet of Secretary Hand.

INTRODUCTION

Exploring source material used to be thought of as only to be practised by an elite of postgraduate students doing 'research'. During the last 30 years, however, adult local historians with very varied educational backgrounds have shown themselves capable of reading and using original records. More recently, local and family history based on primary sources has, with profit, been incorporated into the work of schoolchildren of different ages. The new General Certificate of Secondary Education (GCSE) will undoubtedly lead to an increase in the study of original documents in school history, and make it an acknowledged part of the syllabus. The 'national criteria' for History in GCSE contain the following aims: 'that candidates' knowledge is rooted in an understanding of the nature and the use of historical evidence', and that 'essential study skills' shall be developed, 'such as the ability to locate and extract information from *primary* and secondary sources' (my italics).

Such admirable aims are easier to express than to achieve in practice, as many teachers know. Before the student can work on primary sources, it is necessary to read old handwritings. Practical help is necessary for both school-teachers and pupils, as well as for family and local historians. If a primary source is to be used it must be read correctly and accurately transcribed. Muddling through can be misleading. In the 19th-century printed edition of the Hundred Rolls of 1279, an entry for the village of Burwell in Cambridgeshire lists a local landlord as the nunnery of OKACERIF. The nunnery was actually CHATERIS. An appreciation of how capital *C* and lower-case *h*, *t* and *s* were written, even in the 16th century, will make clear how the transcriber blundered. Local historians wasted much time trying to find a place called Okacerif before they realised the error made by the 19th-century transcriber.

The pamphlet which is reprinted here, with some minor improvements, is intended to help the beginner read the more commonly available documents written between the 16th and 18th centuries, when the majority of documents were written in English. For the medieval period, students have to struggle not only with difficult handwriting but also with Latin. However, these problems can be confronted with the help of books such as *The Handwriting of English Documents* by L. C. Hector (Kohler & Coombes, 1980), *Medieval Local Records* by K. C. Newton (The Historical Association, 1971), *Examples of English Handwriting 1150-1750* by H. E. P. Grieve (Essex Record Office, 1959) and *Latin for Local History* by Eileen A. Gooder (Longmans, 1961). Latin was used until 1733 for certain legal documents, court rolls for example. Quite often an English version or summary has survived, and during the Commonwealth period English was universal for all documents. This means that a 'crib' for the highly standardised phraseology of court rolls can usually be found for those who know no Latin.

In learning how to read and transcribe a document it is sensible to follow certain procedures. A transcript is a copy of a document in which the old handwriting is reproduced as accurately as possible in modern handwriting or in typed form. From the very start, strong self-discipline must be exercised. THE BEGINNER MUST READ A DOCUMENT SLOWLY, LETTER BY LETTER. Ordinarily the eye skips and 'guesses' letters and even words. If the reader does this when learning, he will not progress far, for several letters are misleadingly like quite different letters in the modern alphabet. When a letter cannot be identified for certain, make a dash or put alternative letters one above the other. Only after several lines have been transcribed, should you go back to work out some of the more difficult letters by a process of elimination. Letters which were difficult to read may be identified if found in more than one word. At this stage, but not before, it may be helpful to guess at unidentified words. This is only legitimate if the guess is checked: every guessed-at letter must be found in the manuscript, and every stroke in the manuscript accounted for as part of a letter. It is only too easy to imagine an incorrect word which seems to fit the context, and to deceive oneself into seeing the desired letters when they are not there! Remember that until the 18th century the spelling, even of highly literate people, was not standardised and that many people used local dialect which they spelt phonetically.

Two different alphabets reproduced on pages 4 and 16 introduce the reader to the variety of hands which can be found in English documents of the 16th and 17th centuries. The two main kinds were the Secretary Hand, 'a universally acceptable style ... a handwriting for the ordinary man', and the Court Hand 'extensively used by lawyers and their clerks' (L. C. Hector, *op. cit.*, pp. 57 and 63). The beginner does not need to be too concerned about the differences. After all, handwriting was and is individual and the writers of Secretary Hand, in particular, sometimes followed their own bent. The learner needs to identify the nearest that can be got to the highest common factor, so to say, of each letter. L. C. Hector's book, and *Elizabethan Handwriting 1500-1650* by Giles E. Dawson and Laetitia Kennedy-Skipton (Phillimore, 1981) can be consulted when a level of expertise is reached. Useful introductions for the beginner are *How to Read Local Archives 1550-1700* by F. G. Emmison (The Historical Association, 1967) and *A Secretary Hand ABC Book* by Alf Ison (Alf Ison, 20 Boundary Close, Tilehurst, Reading RG3 5ER).

Capital letters tend to reflect individual idiosyncracies. The best way to identify the capital letters used in a particular document is by elimination and by comparison with examples in the alphabets printed on pages 4 and 16. In what follows each letter of the alphabet is commented on in turn. The concentration is on the lower-case (smaller) letters, and on the more common difficulties met in reading. Although modern letters are reproduced in their printed form, it is their handwritten forms to which reference is being made.

THE ALPHABET

a was often written like a modern *a*, but sometimes the two parts of the letter are separated so that it looks like a modern *oi* without a dot. Occasionally small *a* was written like a curved capital *A* but without its crosspiece.

b was like modern *b*.

c is a most confusing letter, because it was written like a modern *r* and is often misread as *r*.
Capital *C* looks like a hot cross bun with the north-west quarter of the outer rim missing.

d, when carefully written, looks like a printed *d* tipped to the left. When running hand was written, the stroke was looped to save time, and can also lean markedly to the left.

e is another difficult letter to learn. It looks like a squashed version of a running *d* or *b* – the letters can be confused. What appears to be quite a different way of writing *e*, one shallow saucer on top of another, was produced by emphasising the down strokes of the pen and omitting the up and over strokes.

f was written like a modern printed *f* but with the tail below the line; this is how it can be distinguished from a *t*. When written in running hand both the tail and the top were looped and the letter was crossed. There was no capital *F*; two small *f*s were used. So it is a mistake to think that Francis and ffrancis, for example, were different spellings.

g needs to be looked at carefully, for it can easily be taken for *y*. It was written with a curved *u* base on top of which a straight line was drawn from left to right, usually sticking out to the right. The tail was usually, but not always, drawn straight down and then curved to the left.

h is most easily identifiable by the enormous flourish given to its tail below the line. This was not omitted, even when the writer in a hurry drew only one loop, instead of two, above the line. The result looks nothing like a modern *h*, and its shape should be looked at carefully.

i and *j* were interchangeable. The small letter was written like a modern *i*; the form of the capital was between a modern capital *I* and *J*.
It would seem sensible, when transcribing, to write the modern letters, but many scholars always transcribe the lower case as *i* while differentiating the capitals.

k looks like something between a *b* and a modern *k* with its kick horizontal.

l was like modern *l*.

m and *n* retain something from the medieval form: the strokes were joined not at the top by a curve but from bottom left to top right by a straight line. Such letters were called minims, since the word 'minim' in a medieval hand would have consisted of 10 identical downward strokes joined by nine diagonal upward strokes.

o was *o*. Two *o*s together often share a side, and look rather like a *w*.

p requires concentration; it was more like a printed than a modern handwritten *p*, but the part of the letter above the line could be divided, as the Secretary Hand *a* sometimes was.

q was reasonably like a modern *q*.

r had its downward and upward strokes separated; it sometimes looked like a modern *w*, but it could be written like an old-fashioned *e*, or like a *z*, especially when used as a superscript letter and in contractions.

s was written in several ways. At the beginning and in the middle of words it was written in a long form exactly like a Secretary Hand *f* but not crossed. Final *s* was usually written like a *6* leaning to the right. A great many words ended with a silent *e* as in modern French, so plurals in *es* were common. There was a separate symbol for final *es* or *is*; it looks like a modern *e* with its tail lengthened and sprawling below the line.

t was like a modern printed *t*; it can be confused with Secretary Hand *c* or with *f*.

u and *v* were used interchangeably, like *i* and *j*, but there were different forms for both capital and small letters. *Unmoved* might have been written *unmoued* or *vnmoved* or in any mixture, but it would seem rather pedantic to transcribe this in anything but the correct modern forms.

u was written like a modern *u*, but is easily confused with *n*.

v was written differently. In the most common form the pen travelled up the right hand side of the *v* and turned to the left across the top in a straight or curved line.

8

w (double *u/v*) consisted of a Secretary Hand *v* to the left of which part of another *v* was added. Unlike the modern *w* the left hand half of the letter was joined at the top instead of the bottom. Both *w* and *v* can often be identified because they frequently begin with a great flourish from above, which makes them look like the first letter of a word; the second half of the *w* is often fatter and rounded.
w can easily be misread as two letters.

x when written in running hand had a tail curving below the line from the bottom of the left hand cross; this can sometimes be confused with a hurried *h* or *p*.

y was written like a Secretary Hand *v* with a tail which bent first to the left and then curved to the right. It can most easily be distinguished from *g* by the straight line across its top; in a *y* this never had a projection to the right as it had in a *g*, and it was usually less horizontal than in a *g*.

z was not too different from a modern handwritten *z*.

LIGATURES AND CONTRACTIONS

In an age before shorthand or typing, economy in writing was achieved by using a kind of speedwriting, for example by running letters together as ligatures, and by adopting standard abbreviations or contractions. Among the commonest ligatures were

ch   ss

sh

th   ff

st

The most frequent form of contraction consisted of omitting letters and drawing a line above the word: *tenements* was written *ten̄ts*. Often the writer was too lazy to lift his pen to make this line, so he continued in an upward curve from the end of the last letter. Something like a French circumflex accent also came to indicate omitted letters.

The letter with which contractions are most often associated is *p*. *p* followed by a vowel and *r* was shown by an horizontal line through the stem of the *p*, or by an upward curve from the tail of the *p*, to the left, which turned back across the tail just below the line.

or   par, per, por

p followed by *r* and then by a vowel was shown in different ways:

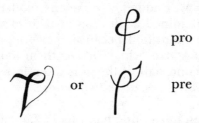

pro

or pre

    Writers did not always use these contractions correctly, so what ought to be *por* or *per* could be *pro* or *pre* or vice-versa.

    The other important form of contraction was the superscript letter, written above the line, which tells the reader that some letters before it have been omitted. It survives when we write 9th for *ninth*; we ought, incidentally, to write *Mr* as M^r.

    z or ε A superscript *r* commonly indicated an omitted *u*, as in *Savio^z* which should be transcribed as *Savio[u]r*.

The most common superscript was in familiar short words like w^t or w^{th} = w[i]th, w^{ch} = w[hi]ch.

When *that* or *the* or *them* was abbreviated, an old Anglo-Saxon letter called the 'thorn', written at first more like a modern *y*, was used for *th*; but soon thorn was written like the Secretary Hand *y*. The best modern practice is to transcribe thorn as *th*, not as *y* which was the habit of older scholars. So y^t is *th[a]t* and *ye* is *the*, NOT *ye*. But remember that there is a word 'ye', meaning 'you' in the plural, spelt with a real *y*! Incidentally, *y* was often written instead of *i*, particularly in words like *if* and *it* which should be transcribed as *yf, yt*.

    When making a transcript it is necessary to show that there was a contraction in the original. This is done by putting brackets round the letters omitted: so M^r ought to be transcribed as *M[aste]r*, w^t as *w[i]t[h]* and p*ish* as *p[ar]ish*. This is the proper way to transcribe.

    Capitals and numerals should be transcribed as in the original manuscript. Abbreviations like *etc* and *viz* need not be extended.

      the ampersand (abbreviation of 'and') should be transcribed &.

But when using such transcripts in writing history, quoting from a document, the writer may modernise anything, provided he is consistent and lets the reader know what practice he is following.

INVENTORY OF ROWLAND BEAMONT OF HITCHIN, HERTFORDSHIRE, 1640

(Reproduced by permission of the County Record Office, Hertford, HCRO 10 HW 127)

The Inventorye of all the moveable goodes[1]
debtes and Chattelles
of Rowland Beamont late of Hitchin in the
Countye of
Hertforde Tayler deceased made the xxij[th]
[sic][2] daye of
Julye Anno do[mi]ni 1640 Praysed by John Hurst
sen[ior][3] and
James Turner sen[ior]

In the Hall
Inprimis[4] one Table, Fower[5] Joyned Stooles,[6] one
Cobarde, with on[7] paynted Clothe on it, Fower
Chayres, Six Coshions, two paynted Clothes, one   xlj[s]
payre of Cobbyrons, one pothanger, one payre of
Belhouse,[8] one payre of Tongs, one Fyreshovell
one gredyron, one spitt, and one fallinge table

In the Chamber
It[e]m one Joyned Bedstede, one Coverlitt, one
Greene blankett, one Fetherbed, one Flockbed,   iij[li][10]
one olde Matteris, one Strawbed Fower boulsters   xiij[s]
and Three Pillows[9]

It[e]m one old Table, one Cheste, one box, three
Cofers
one Woollen Wheele, one Lynnyn Wheele, one   xxv[s]
Clothe baskett, two Chayres, one little Fosser[11] and
Certayne paynted Clothes

REFERENCES

1. Note the *-es* symbol at the end of three words in this line. It should be transcribed as *-es* rather than *-s*. As with all abbreviations, these 'extended' letters can simply be added without acknowledgement (as above), or put inside square brackets to show that the transcriber has actually interpreted an abbreviation symbol (see line 2 of transcript on p. 13).
2. [sic] meaning 'thus' is used to show that the scribe used [th] instead of [nd] This was because he was thinking orally and not visually, and saying to himself 'two and twentieth'.
3. Note the abbreviation symbol looking like a shepherd's crook. This was used to shorten the word 'sen[ior]'. Another clearer example appears on the next line.
4. The Latin 'inprimis' or 'imprimis' means 'firstly' or 'at first'.
5. At the beginning of a word, two small *f*s are transcribed as one capital F. The spelling of 'fower' reflects local dialect.
6. Note how the two *o*s in 'Stooles' merge into each other.
7. 'One' is quite often spelt 'on' or even 'wun'.
8. A good example of the importance of *saying* a word, in order to understand it, and of not being put off by the spelling!
9. To this scribe there is little difference between a capital and lower-case *p*. This example does, however, seem slightly larger than most.
10. The letters *li* with an abbreviation symbol signify the Latin *libra* meaning pound (money).
11. A 'fosser' is a kind of coffer or chest (see 'forcer' in *OED*).

PUNCTUATION

Some documents have no punctuation for many, many lines. Punctuation was most irregular and unsystematic. There were, in fact, very few punctuation marks in use. The most common indication of a break was an oblique stroke. The comma first appeared in the 16th century. Round brackets were used both for parentheses and, sometimes, as inverted commas are used today. A transcript should be faithful to the original. In preparing a document for publication modern punctuation can be introduced, BUT with inadequate punctuation in the original the sense is not always obvious. The student should be alert for ambiguities.

NUMERALS

Roman numerals, in which letters stood for numbers, were still in common use.

1 = j   2 = ij   3 = iij   4 = iiij   5 = v

i and j both represented 1; the last 1 was always represented by j.

6 = vj   7 = vij   9 = ix   10 = x   11 = xj   and so on.

iv for 4 and xiv for 14 only appear in later documents.

15 = xv   20 = xx   40 = xl   50 = l   100 = C   500 = D   1000 = M

Pounds, shillings and pence were indicated by superscript letters. The £ sign was $\bar{\text{li}}$, short for *libra*, the Latin word for a pound. In fact our modern £ sign is a capital L with the contraction line, to show 'ibra' omitted, drawn above the bottom loop. The shilling sign was the final *s*, symbol for *solidus*; the pence sign was *d*, for *denarius*; they were two Roman coins.

Since counting was done in scores (20), a large number might be put into numerals as a number of scores. The sum total of an inventory might be written as $\text{vj}^{xx}\text{vj}^{\bar{\text{li}}}\ \text{v}^{s}$ iiij^{d}, which was spoken as six score and six pounds (i.e. £126), five shillings and four pence.

There was a 4^d coin called a groat, which was useful because so many calculations were done in marks or parts of marks. There was never a coin worth a mark, but people made gifts and valued objects in that unit which was two-thirds of a £, that is $13^s\ 4^d$; half a mark was $6^s\ 8^d$. *Di*, short for the Latin *dimidium*, was a half, but *ob*, short for the Latin *obulus* from the Green coin, was $\frac{1}{2}^d$; *qu*, short for *quarteria*, was $\frac{1}{4}^d$.

Local historians will frequently find land measurements in the sources which they use. Square measurements were in acres, roods and perches, abbreviated to *a, r, p*. 40 perches = 1 rood; 4 roods = 1 acre. Confusion can arise because a perch is also a measure of length: rod, pole and perch were different names for the same distance, which originally varied by custom but became standardised at 5½ yards.

GLEBE TERRIER OF DALHAM, SUFFOLK, 1613
(Suffolk Record Office, Bury St Edmunds, E14/4/1)

Dalha[m][1] 1613

A Terriar of the Glebe Land[es][2] and
howses belonginge to the Rectorye or
p[ar]sonage[3] of dalha[m] dated the thyrd daye
of Januarye[4] A[nn]o 1613

Inp[ri]mis[5] one mansion or dwellynge howse one
backhowse &[6] two[7] howses for necessary uses[8]
one orchard & one gardine[9]

It[e]m one barne one stable & one Close of
pasture Contayninge by estimation one Acer
nere adioyninge to the sayd barne & stable

It[e]m one pece of medowe Laye ground and
arable[10] Lyenge together nere unto moulton
Contayninge by estimation Six acers
the medowe liethe \at/[11] both[][12] end[es] \of/ the
medowe of
George Traycye gent[leman] & Co[n]tayneth by
estimation
v Rodes the one seyde abutte the upon the broke
toward[es] the Weste & the one end abutteth
upon the medow of the forsayd Gorge[13] Traycie
toward[es] the Easte & the other ende upone the
sayd
broke toward[es] |.the.|[14] moulton & toward[es]
the north
& the Arable \land/ abutteth upon the Landes
of dyvers menes toward[es] the East & the
one end abbutth [sic] upon the foresayd broke
toward[es]
the north & the other end toward[es] the East

REFERENCES

1. The bar above *a* is an abbreviation sign, showing that the final *m* has been dropped. Note that it is virtually impossible to distinguish a capital from a lower-case *d* (compare with line 4).
2. Note the *-es* symbol.
3. Note the symbol for *par-*.
4. The *n* and *u* in 'Januarye' are written identically, but the context enables us to distinguish them correctly.
5. The Latin 'inprimis' or 'imprimis' means 'firstly' or 'at first'. Note that the scribe has wrongly used the *par* symbol, instead of *pre* (actually for *pri* in this context).
6. It is better to transcribe the ampersand as &, so that we can distinguish it from a fully written 'and'.
7. There appears to be a meaningless comma here, or is it a flourish from the ampersand below?
8. Note how a lower-case *u* can begin with an exaggerated flourish.
9. Notice how some lines that would have ended in blank spaces are filled up with horizontal lines.
10. With this script, it is sometimes difficult, or impossible, to distinguish capitals from lower-case letters. Is this 'Arable' or 'arable'?
11. This convention using oblique strokes distinguishes an insertion into the original text. Transcribers should certainly distinguish insertions by this, or some other suitable convention.
12. Does the word 'both' end with an *e* or just a blot or crossing-out?
13. Notice that 'George' is now spelt without its first *e*.
14. This convention of vertical lines and dots distinguishes a deletion from the original text. Transcribers should certainly distinguish deletions by this, or some other suitable convention.

DATES

Dates, when expressed numerically, were frequently assumed to be abbreviations of Latin, not English words. Latin nouns change their endings for different cases; the ablative case was used for dates. So the following ending would normally be found:

1st = 1º, for primo   6th = 6to, for sexto
2nd = 2do, for secundo   7th = 7mo, for septimo
3rd = 3º, for tertio   8th = 8º, for octavo
4th = 4to, for quarto   9th = 9º, for nono
5th = 5to, for quinto   10th = 10º, for decimo

Dates were not always given in the modern fashion. There were two alternatives: using a Saint's day instead of the day of the month; and using the year of the monarch's reign for the calendar year. *Handbook of Dates for Students of English History* by C. R. Cheney (Royal Historical Society, 1970) is the essential reference book for interpreting these. It must be remembered that a monarch's reign does not correspond with the calendar year, but runs from the date of accession to the date of death. Mary I died and Elizabeth I came to the throne on 17 November 1558. So the first year of Elizabeth I's reign extended from 17 November 1558 to 16 November 1559 inclusive. 1 December 1 Elizabeth was 1 December 1558, while 1 March 1 Elizabeth was 1 March 1559.

One reason for using the 'regnal year', as it was called, may have been to avoid the confusions which gathered around the calendar year. Only on 1 January 1752 did England return to the Roman practice of beginning each year on 1 January; the Scots had made the change on 1 January 1600, and much of Europe earlier in the 16th century. Before these changes the new year was assumed to begin on 25 March, Lady Day, the day of the Annunciation. From the time when change took place in Europe until 1752, English dates between 1 January and 24 March were sometimes given a double indication: Charles I was executed on 30 January 164⁸⁄₉. The bottom date is the one which accords with our usage. Whenever a document, of an earlier date than 1752, has only one year given and it falls between 1 January and 24 March inclusive, the student must modernise the year by adding one. To ensure that one does not forget whether this has been done, and make a double adjustment, it may be sensible in taking notes to give the double indication.

There is, unfortunately, an additional complication. In 1582 Pope Gregory XIII replaced the Julian calendar, introduced by Julius Caesar in 45 B.C., with the Gregorian calendar. This was intended to remedy the growing divergence between the calendar year and the solar year by reducing slightly the number of leap years; in only one in four future centuries was the first year to be a leap year. But a discrepancy already existed and to remove this the calendar had to catch up with the solar year. In 1582, therefore, 15 October followed immediately after 4 October, there being a jump of 10 days. This adjustment was made at different times by different countries: in 1752 in England 14 September followed 2 September; in Russia the 1917 Revolution occurred on what was then 25 October but is now celebrated as though it had been 7 November, the date according to the Gregorian calendar. One peculiarly British institution commemorates the old order in a confused way. In most countries the Finance Minister opens his year on 1 January, but in Britain the Chancellor of the Exchequer's 'budget speech' used to be made on 5 April, and the Income Tax year still begins on 6 April. Before 1752 budget day was on 25 March, the first day of the year. The addition of 11 days in 1752 brought this forward to 5 April. For some extraordinary reason British budgetary practice accepted the adjustment in the day but not in the beginning of the New Year.

ACCOUNT BOOK OF HENGRAVE PARK, SUFFOLK
(Suffolk Record Office, Bury St Edmunds, HA 528/5730/113)

A Booke of accompt for all[e][1] kynd[es] of Deare put in to Hengrave   1587 p[ar]ke[2] w[hi]ch parke was fynished at my hellmas [sic][3] in Anno

In this yeare (1587) A whyt soore[4] was geven me by S[i]r Clement hygham knyght and was kylled, by the Ladye kytson, the iiijth Daye of September |.in the.|[5] in the yeare 1592. And wayed in his skyne savinge his hedd xvij stonne,[6] the wayte of him beinge brawken upp w[i]th his showlders was xj stonne ix ll'[7]   /the sto[n]ne xiiij l[bs]

REFERENCES

1. Double *ls* at the ends of words often have an abbreviation symbol over them. This became a mere habit, but originally indicated the final and normally silent *e*.
2. Note the symbol for *par-*.
3. The editorial [*sic*] appears here to show that the normal *c* or *g* in the word Michaelmas was not used by the scribe.
4. A 'sore' was a male deer or buck in its fourth year (see *OED*).
5. These symbols can be used to show words which have been crossed out.
6. This word could perhaps be transcribed as 'sto*u*ne', because *n* and *u* are indistinguishable, and the *u* sound was certainly more common in Elizabethan speech than it is today.
7. The two *ls* with an abbreviation sign here signify the Latin *librae*, plural of *libra*, meaning pound weight (or lb/s). At this point, other transcribers might have preferred to put [librae] or [lbs] or [pounds]. As the marginal note indicates, a stone was the equivalent of 14 lbs.

A general Alphabet of the Old Law Hands.

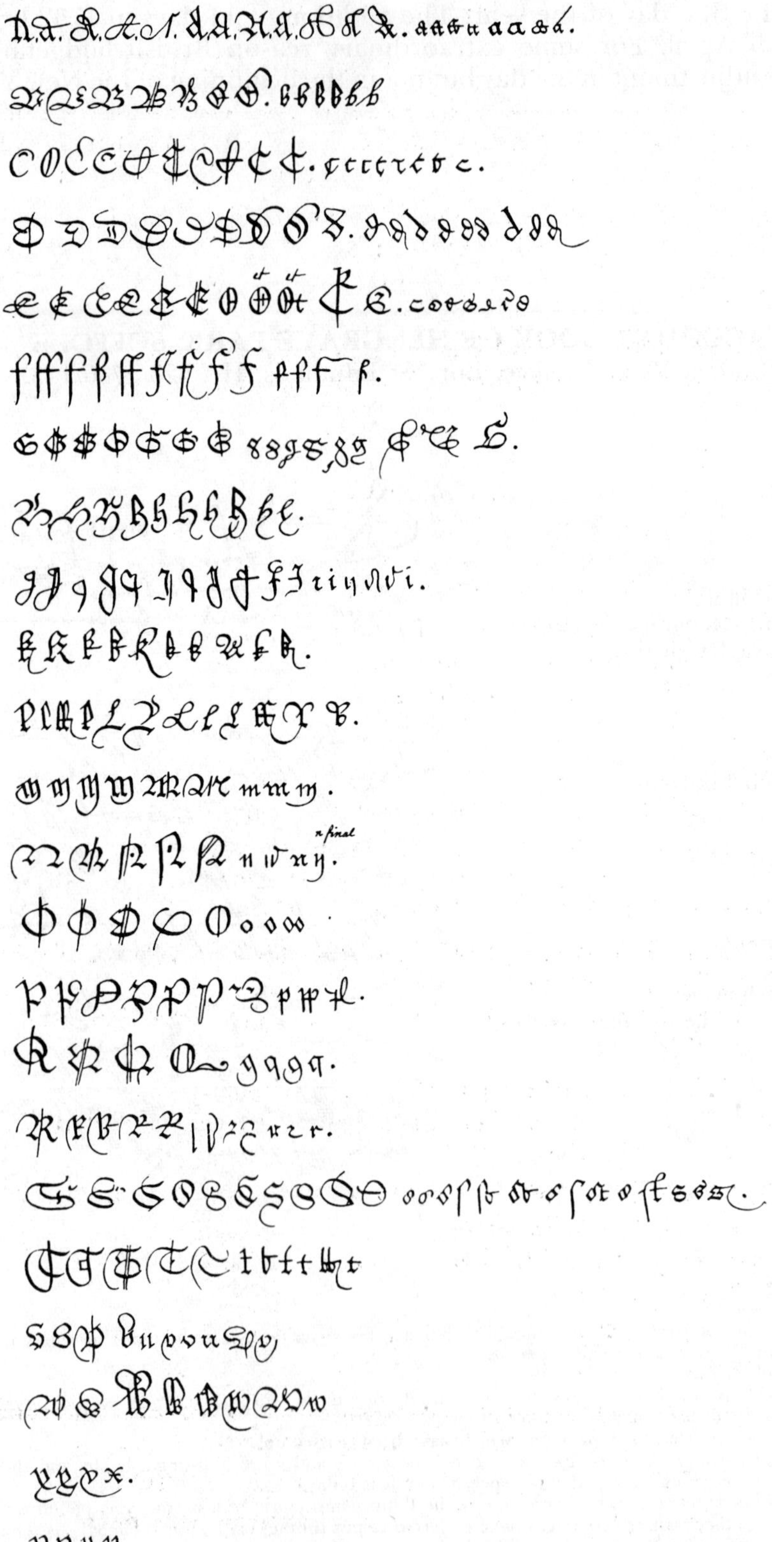

Alphabet of Court Hands.